Original title:

Dancing on Dream Clouds

Copyright © 2024 Creative Arts Management OÜ

All rights reserved.

Author: Arabella Whitmore

ISBN HARDBACK: 978-9916-90-518-0

ISBN PAPERBACK: 978-9916-90-519-7

Shifting Perspective Amongst Cosmic Veils

Stars whisper secrets in the night,
Galaxies swirl in a dance of light.
Time bends softly, stretching the view,
Infinite wonders, both old and new.

Nebulas bloom like dreams on the edge,
Colorful canvases, nature's pledge.
Each twinkling orb tells stories untold,
Mysteries wrapped in stardust and gold.

Planets revolve in a cosmic sway,
Orbiting truths that guide our way.
A heartbeat echoes in the vastness near,
In every silence, the cosmos hears.

Eyes to the heavens, we strive to see,
Shifting perspectives, setting minds free.
Amongst the veils of the universe spun,
We find our place, a journey begun.

Floating Hearts in Boundless Space

In the dark where dreams align,
Hearts like stars, they weave and twine.
A canvas vast, soft whispers soar,
Infinity calls from every shore.

Each heartbeat echoes in the night,
A cosmic dance, pure delight.
Floating freely, a gentle sigh,
Love glimmers bright in the endless sky.

Whispers of Celestial Waltz

Galaxies spin, a graceful trance,
Whispers float in cosmic dance.
Moonbeams flicker soft and light,
Painting dreams in silver night.

Stardust swirls, a tapestry,
Moments wrapped in mystery.
Hearts align as planets glide,
In this waltz, we must abide.

Chasing Stardust Footsteps

Echoes of stars beckon us near,
Chasing trails without fear.
Footsteps chart a pathway bright,
Through the velvet of the night.

Each spark a hint of a tale,
Across the skies, we set sail.
In the shimmer, we rediscover,
The magic hidden, like no other.

Serendipity in the Sky

Clouds drift softly, tales unfold,
In every shadow, wonders untold.
Serendipity wraps us tight,
Painting moments with pure light.

Rainbows arch and colors blend,
A myriad of dreams to send.
In these skies, we find our way,
Serendipity leads the day.

Swaying with Cosmic Whispers

In the hush of night so deep,
Stars hum secrets, softly sweep.
Galaxies twirl, a dance divine,
Eternal echoes, hearts entwine.

Moonbeams brush the velvet sky,
Whispers of dreams that drift and fly.
In twilight's glow, we find our peace,
Embracing the night as worries cease.

Drifting with the Aurora

Colors weave in silent flight,
Dancing ribbons, pure delight.
Underneath the luminous veil,
Hearts take wing, they do not fail.

Each hue a story, pure and bright,
Wrapped in dreams that chase the light.
Nature's canvas, bold and grand,
Together we drift, hand in hand.

The Unseen Rhythm of the Cosmos

Beyond the stars, a pulse awaits,
A heartbeat that reverberates.
Time and space in harmony,
We are notes in symphony.

Gravity binds yet sets us free,
Whirling through eternity.
In this dance, we find our role,
A cosmic tale that fills the soul.

Winding through Celestial Gardens

Petals of stardust gently fall,
Each a whisper, nature's call.
In gardens vast, we wander slow,
Finding truths that gently flow.

Planets bloom in vibrant hues,
Sowing dreams that we can choose.
Among the orbs, we seek our path,
Bathing in the universe's bath.

Waltzing with the Winds of Fantasy

In twilight's embrace, we sway and dip,
The world around us begins to flip.
Whispers of dreams twirl through the air,
In this dance of hearts, we lose our care.

Stars like confetti fall from above,
Each twinkle a promise, a tale of love.
With every step, our spirits soar high,
Waltzing with whimsy beneath the sky.

A Serenade in the Sky

Soft melodies drift on the evening breeze,
Carried by whispers through swaying trees.
Clouds become vessels of dreams that roam,
A serenade sweet, inviting us home.

The sun bows low, painting skies with gold,
Every note a secret that longs to be told.
In this symphony, our hearts resonate,
Capturing moments that time can't abate.

Spirals of Illusion and Air

In spirals we dance, through shadows and light,
Where visions ignite in the depth of the night.
Reality bends, in a twist and a spin,
Embracing the magic that dwells deep within.

A fleeting illusion, the world takes a turn,
In whispers of wonder, our souls start to yearn.
Floating through dreams, we chase after gleams,
Each breath a new chapter, unfurling our seams.

Steps in the Moonlit Mist

Through moonlit paths where shadows play,
We wander softly, lost in the sway.
The mist wraps around like a silken thread,
Guiding our footsteps with secrets unsaid.

Each twinkle above wraps us in its glow,
We dance with the echoes of thoughts that flow.
With every step, the night whispers sweet,
In this misty embrace, our hearts gently meet.

Undulating Above the Horizon

Waves of gold kiss the sky,
As the sun begins to rise.
Echoes of dawn's soft sigh,
Painted clouds in sweet disguise.

Mountains stretch and stand so tall,
Guardians of the waking light.
Nature's chorus starts to call,
Embracing day, bidding night.

Fields of green wave in the breeze,
Whispering secrets of the day.
The earth breathes a moment's ease,
In the light where shadows play.

Moments drift like softest dreams,
Flowing gently, never still.
Time, it dances in moonbeams,
Awakening the heart's sweet thrill.

The Celestial Cha-Cha

Stars twirl in the vast expanse,
Galaxies spin a timeless dance.
Planets glimmer, a radiant trance,
In this cosmic, wild romance.

Comets streak like dreams at night,
Tales of wanderers, bold and bright.
Moonlight bathes the world in white,
A sonnet sung in silver light.

Nebulas swirl in colors grand,
A palette crafted by unseen hand.
Twilight beckons to the land,
As stardust falls like grains of sand.

Eternal rhythms pulse and thrum,
The universe beats like a drum.
In this space where wonders come,
The celestial cha-cha has begun.

Undulating Above the Horizon

Waves of gold kiss the sky,
As the sun begins to rise.
Echoes of dawn's soft sigh,
Painted clouds in sweet disguise.

Mountains stretch and stand so tall,
Guardians of the waking light.
Nature's chorus starts to call,
Embracing day, bidding night.

Fields of green wave in the breeze,
Whispering secrets of the day.
The earth breathes a moment's ease,
In the light where shadows play.

Moments drift like softest dreams,
Flowing gently, never still.
Time, it dances in moonbeams,
Awakening the heart's sweet thrill.

The Celestial Cha-Cha

Stars twirl in the vast expanse,
Galaxies spin a timeless dance.
Planets glimmer, a radiant trance,
In this cosmic, wild romance.

Comets streak like dreams at night,
Tales of wanderers, bold and bright.
Moonlight bathes the world in white,
A sonnet sung in silver light.

Nebulas swirl in colors grand,
A palette crafted by unseen hand.
Twilight beckons to the land,
As stardust falls like grains of sand.

Eternal rhythms pulse and thrum,
The universe beats like a drum.
In this space where wonders come,
The celestial cha-cha has begun.

A Serenade Among the Dreamscapes

Whispers of night in soft embrace,
Gently weave through the quiet space.
Stars are scattered, lace in place,
Dreams take form, a fleeting chase.

Moonlit paths call the soul to roam,
In gardens where the shadows comb.
Every heart finds a place called home,
In the realms where visions roam.

Clouds like cotton, drifting high,
Underneath the velvet sky.
Time is lost, a gentle sigh,
As lullabies to stardust fly.

In a world where dreams can bloom,
Magic dwells in each small room.
Catch a song, let the heart consume,
In this serenade, forever loom.

Whirling with Gossamer Spirits

In the twilight where shadows play,
Gossamer spirits serenade the day.
Dancing light on branches sway,
Whirls of magic, come what may.

Breezes carry laughter's tune,
Through the glow of a silvery moon.
Softly wrapped in night's soft swoon,
Nature's heart beats, a sweet boon.

Mystic tales in whispers twine,
Veils of mist the stars align.
Every moment, a fleeting sign,
With every breath, the world divine.

Embrace the flutter, join the whirl,
Let the spirits spin and twirl.
In their dance, let your heart unfurl,
As life becomes a glimmering pearl.

Elysian Steps Across the Firmament

In twilight's glow we tread so light,
Beneath the stars that softly bright.
Each step a dance in cosmic streams,
We chase the whispers of our dreams.

With every breath the night unfolds,
A story woven, gently told.
The skies adorned with shades of grace,
In this vast realm, we find our place.

Above, the moon, a watchful eye,
As constellations weave and fly.
We wander through this endless night,
On Elysian steps, in pure delight.

Celestial Rhymes on Airy Wings

In the quiet hush of morning light,
Birds sing songs that take to flight.
Their melodies on breezes twine,
In union with the stars, they shine.

Each note a spark, a fleeting dream,
Floating softly on the stream.
The sky itself hums a tune,
Beneath the watchful, silver moon.

In these moments, hearts align,
With earthly joys and love divine.
We soar above, on airy wings,
In the embrace that freedom brings.

Cascading Melodies in the Stratosphere

Through clouds of white, the echoes play,
Cascading notes that drift away.
They weave a tapestry of sound,
In lofty heights, where dreams are found.

The sun breaks through, a golden ray,
Illuminating trails of gray.
With gentle winds, the harmonies,
Dance in the warmth of summer's breeze.

A symphony of whispers rise,
Like laughter shared beneath the skies.
In every drop of melody,
We find the joy of being free.

Gliding on Soft Whispers

On softest whispers, we take flight,
Into the depths of endless night.
The world below fades into dreams,
As starlit paths flow like silver streams.

We glide along the velvet air,
With every breath, we lose our care.
In twilight's arms, our spirits soar,
Where silence speaks and minds explore.

The whispers guide us, soft and low,
Through realms of light where breezes flow.
In this embrace, we learn to see,
The beauty of our souls set free.

Glide through the Veils of Twilight

In dusk's embrace, shadows dance,
Whispers of secrets, take their chance.
Stars awaken, softly gleam,
As the night unveils its dream.

Moonlit paths weave through the night,
Guiding lost souls toward the light.
Veils of twilight gently fall,
In silence, we heed their call.

Breezes carry tales of yore,
Through the woods, an ancient lore.
The horizon blurs with hues,
As night cloaks the world anew.

Glide with grace on starlit flow,
Where time and dreams together grow.
Each moment drips like precious dew,
In twilight's arms, we are made true.

Footprints on Gossamer Skies

Above the clouds, dreams take flight,
Painting the heavens with pure light.
Footprints trace where angels tread,
In soft whispers, words unsaid.

Colors blend in a dance so fine,
Gossamer threads of the divine.
Each step a story, softly spun,
Underneath the watchful sun.

Hearts soar high, tethered to hope,
In this realm, we learn to cope.
The boundless sky holds secrets sweet,
In gossamer dreams, our souls meet.

Together we weave through endless flight,
Creating our dawn from the night.
With every breath, we leave our mark,
Footprints glowing, a spark in the dark.

The Rhythm of Dreamscapes

In lands unknown, our spirits roam,
Sketching life's tale away from home.
The rhythm sways, a gentle beat,
In every pulse, our dreams repeat.

Mountains rise, valleys sink low,
Where time is lost, and rivers flow.
Dancing shadows in twilight's tune,
As hearts align with the silver moon.

Echoes whisper through the trees,
Carried softly on the breeze.
We spin in circles, never end,
In dreamscapes where our souls ascend.

With every heartbeat, we repose,
Where time dissolves and passion grows.
In this embrace, we lose our way,
Finding life in the break of day.

Embracing the Feathered Horizon

Beyond the edges of our sight,
Feathers float on winds of night.
The horizon stretches, calling clear,
Inviting dreams to gather near.

With every flap, new worlds unfold,
Stories shared, both brave and bold.
Through the air, our spirits soar,
Together we seek, forevermore.

Each feather whispers tales of old,
Wisdom nurtured, stories told.
In twilight hues, horizons blend,
A journey starts, no need to end.

So let us chase where islands drift,
Embracing the sky, a precious gift.
With feathered hearts, we make our vow,
To live the wonder of the now.

Balancing on Fluffy Horizons

In the dawn's soft, golden glow,
We tread on clouds, light as air.
With every step, possibility,
The world dances without a care.

Horizon whispers dreams untold,
Each breath a chance to soar higher.
Balancing hope on wings of gold,
Hearts ignited, souls on fire.

Beneath the sky, we find our way,
Where colors blend in twilight's grace.
With laughter echoing, we play,
On fluffy horizons, we embrace.

Together we chase the mystic light,
In a world where dreams intertwine.
Every shadow fades from sight,
As we dance on this divine line.

Ballet of the Imagination

In twilight's hue, thoughts take flight,
Twisting and turning, a vibrant dance.
Each movement a spark, pure delight,
Imagination paints a trance.

With whispers of dreams softly spun,
A waltz where the ordinary fades.
Every story, a new begun,
In a world where magic invades.

Footfalls light on clouds of thought,
Each leap a chance to break free.
In this ballet, all fears are caught,
As we twirl in pure fantasy.

Together we craft, together we sway,
In a realm of colors and sound.
Imagination leads the way,
In this dance of dreams, unbound.

Ascending the Whispering Stratosphere

Beneath the stars, we raise our gaze,
Whispers of freedom guide our climb.
In the stillness, a shiver amaze,
As we reach for the edge of time.

With every heartbeat, we catch the wind,
Floating on hopes that never cease.
The stratosphere calls, sweetly pinned,
To soar above, in a dance of peace.

Through clouds we weave, like threads of silk,
In a tapestry woven so high.
Each breath is a promise, soft as milk,
In the embrace of the open sky.

Together we rise, beyond the stars,
Letting the universe set us free.
Chasing the light, ignoring the scars,
In this ascent, just you and me.

Curled in the Arms of a Dream

In a gentle dusk, where shadows play,
I find solace in whispers of night.
Curled up softly, as worries sway,
In the arms of a dream, pure and bright.

Each thought a feather, light on my soul,
Floating in realms where time stands still.
In this embrace, I become whole,
Through the silence, I feel the thrill.

Delicate visions dance in my mind,
Like fireflies flickering, weaving delight.
A world unbound, so tender, so kind,
In the arms of a dream, I take flight.

As dawn approaches, I hold on tight,
To the magic of dreams that softly gleam.
In the heartbeat of night, I find my light,
Forever curled in the arms of a dream.

Whispers of Stardust

In the quiet night we dream,
Stars above begin to gleam.
Whispers swirling through the air,
Secrets held without a care.

Galaxies spin in the sky,
Echoes of a distant sigh.
Each glow a wish, softly cast,
Moments linger, shadows fast.

Twinkling gems of ancient light,
Guiding souls through velvet night.
Every sparkle holds a tale,
In the cosmos, we set sail.

So let the stardust pave our way,
Through the night, till break of day.
In the dance of dreams, we find,
The hidden paths of heart and mind.

Cotton Candy Waltz

Swirls of pink in a summer fair,
Laughter dances in the air.
Children twirl beneath the sun,
Chasing dreams, they laugh and run.

Clouds of sugar, soft and sweet,
Melodies of joy repeat.
As they spin around with glee,
Life feels like a symphony.

With each taste, the world turns bright,
Moments blaze in pure delight.
Cotton candy dreams take flight,
In their hearts, the stars ignite.

So let us waltz beneath the sky,
With hearts so light, we soar so high.
In this bliss, we share a glance,
And lose ourselves in a sweet dance.

Chasing Moonbeams

Underneath the silver glow,
Silent waves begin to flow.
Dancing shadows on the ground,
In the night, our dreams are found.

With each step, the stars align,
Whispers soft, a gentle sign.
Chasing beams of pale moonlight,
In their glow, we're infinite.

Every leap, a story told,
In the dark, our hearts are bold.
Floating freely, hand in hand,
In this magical expanse, we stand.

So let the night unfold its grace,
In the moon's tender embrace.
We'll chase the light, our spirits soar,
Forever seeking, forever more.

Floating on Nimbus Wings

Up above in skies so blue,
Floating dreams are made for two.
Clouds like pillows, soft and white,
Carrying hearts towards the light.

With each gust, we drift and glide,
On the breeze, we turn with pride.
Weightless through the azure sea,
In this moment, we are free.

Gentle whispers from the heights,
Sunlit paths and starry nights.
Every breath a sigh of peace,
In this haven, worries cease.

So let us soar on wings of dreams,
Where the world is not what it seems.
Floating on through endless skies,
With love's touch, we shall arise.

Twirling Through Celestial Realms

Stars awaken in the night,
Dancing shadows, pure delight.
Galaxies spin in silent grace,
Twirling dreams in endless space.

Whispers float on cosmic air,
Silken threads beyond compare.
Nebulae glow with gentle might,
Guiding wanderers through the light.

Planets waltz in moonlit streams,
Drawing us into their dreams.
Eclipses paint the skies anew,
A ballet of the vast and true.

In this realm, we lose our care,
Twirling through the stardust rare.
Every heartbeat echoes loud,
In the dance, we're lost, so proud.

Silhouettes Beneath the Aurora

Dancing lights paint the night sky,
Whispers of colors, oh so sly.
Silhouettes in soft shadows sway,
Embraced by the night, they play.

Beneath the aurora's warm embrace,
Pulsing rhythms, a sacred space.
Figures moving in gentle trance,
Caught in nature's lively dance.

Chasing dreams in every hue,
A tapestry of me and you.
Underneath the stars so bright,
Silhouettes lost in pure delight.

With every flicker, hearts ignite,
As we sway in delight tonight.
In this magic, time stands still,
Beneath the aurora's gentle thrill.

A Lullaby of Ethereal Steps

Moonlight spills on shimmering dew,
As spirits gather, soft and true.
Each step echoes a timeless song,
A lullaby where we belong.

In the stillness, whispers blend,
Tales of journeys without end.
Ethereal paths call out our name,
In this dance, we feel no shame.

Winds carry secrets from afar,
Guiding us beneath each star.
Softly swaying, we take flight,
In the embrace of tranquil night.

With every breath, the world slows down,
Lost in motion, we wear no crown.
Together, we find our place,
In the lullaby of soft grace.

Swaying with Celestial Echoes

Clouds drift softly, a gentle sigh,
As constellations light the sky.
In the glimmer of stars alight,
We sway to echoes of the night.

Time stands still in this embrace,
Each moment etched in warm space.
Echoes of ancient tales we hear,
Whispers from the cosmos near.

With every pulse, the universe calls,
Cascading wonders, as twilight falls.
Together we move, hearts in sync,
Connecting through the cosmic link.

In the dance of celestial grace,
We find our rhythm, a sacred place.
Swaying gently with every breath,
In the echoes of life and death.

Dreams Adrift in Weightless Waltz

In twilight hues, we float along,
With whispers soft, where dreams belong.
The stars above, they gently sway,
In weightless grace, they guide our play.

Through lavender skies, we drift and glide,
Each wish a ripple, a gentle tide.
In moonlit beams, we dance so free,
Embracing all we long to be.

As night unfolds a silken thread,
A tapestry of dreams, we're led.
With every turn, the world's a song,
In weightless waltz, we all belong.

With hearts entwined, we find our way,
In dreams adrift, we'll always stay.
Beyond the stars, our spirits soar,
In this sweet dance, forevermore.

Cosmic Ballet of the Heart

In the vast expanse of night's embrace,
Galaxies twirl in a timeless race.
Constellations wink with radiant light,
In cosmic ballet, hearts take flight.

Whirling through stardust, we find our place,
In the rhythm of love, a tender grace.
Celestial whispers in the dark,
Fuel the fire, igniting the spark.

Each twinkle tells a story true,
Of dreams we hold, and hopes anew.
In swirling orbits, our souls entwine,
As the universe sings, we shine.

Together we dance, so wild, so free,
In this cosmic waltz, just you and me.
With every heartbeat, we take a chance,
In the cosmic ballet, we find romance.

Riding the Zephyrs of Imagination

On gentle winds, our visions soar,
Through fragrant fields, we'll wander more.
Imagination's wings, wide and bright,
Will carry us far into the light.

Through valleys of dreams, we leap and bound,
In colors vivid, magic is found.
With every gust, new paths unfold,
On zephyrs sweet, our tales are told.

In whispered breezes, stories ignite,
With echoes of laughter, pure delight.
We ride the winds, through time and space,
In the world of dreams, we find our place.

So hold my hand, let's take this flight,
On imagination's wings, through day and night.
With hearts ablaze and spirits high,
We'll chase the winds beneath the sky.

Ascending with the Spirit of Joy

With each new dawn, the sun ascends,
In golden rays, our hope transcends.
The spirit of joy begins to rise,
Illuminating all with vibrant skies.

Through fields of laughter, we skip along,
In every heartbeat, there's a song.
With every step, we touch the light,
Ascending higher, with pure delight.

In the dance of life, we twirl and spin,
Embracing moments, where dreams begin.
As joy unfurls, like petals in bloom,
We share our light, dispelling gloom.

So come with me, let's soar above,
With the spirit of joy and endless love.
Together we'll climb, hand in hand,
Ascending to heights, so grand and unplanned.

Echoes of Light and Laughter

In the meadow, joy takes flight,
Children's laughter fills the night.
Stars above, twinkling bright,
Echoes dance with pure delight.

Gentle whispers through the trees,
Softly carried on the breeze.
Every heart finds joy that glows,
In harmonious ebb and flow.

Moonlit paths weave dreams anew,
Sparkling moments, tried and true.
Time stands still, in love we bask,
In warm glow, no need to ask.

Hand in hand, we chase the light,
Together, we conquer the night.
As echoes fade, memories cling,
To the joy that laughter brings.

Blissful Pirouettes in the Ether

On whispered winds, spirits twirl,
In rhythm, a cosmic swirl.
Stars align in perfect grace,
A dance of light in timeless space.

Veils of color grace the skies,
Where dreams awaken, softly rise.
Each pirouette, a fleeting kiss,
In this realm of endless bliss.

The universe, a grand ballet,
As stardust swirls and spirits play.
Through shimmering night, we glide,
In the ether, hearts open wide.

Close your eyes, just feel the flight,
In the dance of day and night.
Forever caught in the embrace,
Of blissful pirouettes in space.

A Journey Through Celestial Fields

Through cosmic fields where comets roam,
Time unfurls, we find our home.
Galaxies spin, a bright parade,
In the vastness, dreams are made.

Nebulas blossom, colors blend,
A tapestry that has no end.
With each step, new worlds arise,
As starlit wonders fill our eyes.

Planets hum a gentle tune,
Underneath the watchful moon.
Every heartbeat, light conspires,
To weave our fate with cosmic fires.

Together, we will journey far,
Guided by a single star.
In celestial fields, we will soar,
Exploring realms forever more.

The Art of Cosmic Flight

In silent skies, we stretch our wings,
Soaring high where starlight sings.
The cosmos breathes, a vibrant hue,
As we embrace the boundless blue.

Drifting through the Milky Way,
In dreams, we dance, in dreams, we play.
Each twinkling star, a guiding light,
Leading us through the endless night.

In the art of flight, we are free,
Navigating cosmic sea.
With heart and spirit intertwined,
In the universe, we are enshrined.

On wings of wonder, we unite,
Chasing shadows into light.
The art of flight forever calls,
In the vast expanse, our spirit sprawls.

Spiral of Infinity Above

A spiral twirls in endless flight,
Stars whisper secrets, soft and bright.
Galaxies bloom in cosmic dance,
Time drifts gently in a trance.

Nebulae swirl in colors bold,
Stories of ages yet untold.
Gravity's pull, a tender embrace,
In the vastness, we find our place.

Winds of time, they softly blow,
Through constellations, we learn to flow.
In the tapestry of the night,
Infinity's beauty, pure delight.

A realm where dreams and stars collide,
In the spiral vast, we take our ride.
With every turn, the heart ignites,
In the spiral of infinite heights.

Dreams Dipped in Stardust

Upon the canvas, night unfolds,
Dreams dipped in stardust, tales retold.
Whispers of wishes sparkle bright,
In shadows of the velvet night.

Luminous thoughts like fireflies seem,
Floating through the realms of dream.
Each spark a journey, each wish a call,
In the stardust, we rise and fall.

The moonlight dances on silver streams,
Embracing the echoes of our dreams.
With every heartbeat, the cosmos sways,
Painting our hopes in endless arrays.

In the soft glow, we lose our way,
Yet find our hearts in night's ballet.
Forever lost in this gentle trust,
We live forever, dreams dipped in stardust.

Joyful Circles in the Sky

A circle, bright, in azure blue,
Kites dance freely, skies anew.
In loops of laughter, time stands still,
Joyful circles, a cherished thrill.

Clouds like cotton, soft and white,
Playful shapes in golden light.
With every turn, our spirits rise,
In joyful circles, hearts reprise.

The sun dips low, the day finds peace,
In these circles, we seek release.
Whispers of breezes carry our dreams,
In endless loops, life's sweet themes.

As twilight paints the world in grace,
Joyful circles, our warm embrace.
Underneath the starlit sky,
Together, we twirl, and never say goodbye.

A Waltz Through Weightlessness

In zero-gravity, we feel the light,
A waltz through space, pure delight.
Stars become partners, twirling fine,
In a cosmic dance, hearts entwine.

Floating dreams ignite the night,
Each sway and turn feels so right.
Galactic rhythm, a gentle sway,
We drift through shadows, come what may.

Infinite air beneath our feet,
In weightlessness, life feels sweet.
Hands held tight, we spin and glide,
In this vastness, love won't hide.

Together we float, a timeless scene,
As the universe whispers, soft and keen.
In the ballet of stars, we hear the call,
A waltz through weightlessness, enchanting for all.

The Symphony of Upward Dreams

In the quiet night, hopes take flight,
With whispers soft, they chase the light.
Every star a note, in harmony they gleam,
Creating a score of an upward dream.

Beneath the moon's glow, visions ignite,
Carried on wings, they soar from sight.
In the realm of dreams, where wishes align,
A symphony swells, pure and divine.

Each heartbeat a rhythm, each breath a song,
Together they dance, where we belong.
With courage as chords, and love as the theme,
We rise in the echo of upward dream.

Through valleys of doubt, to mountains of grace,
The melody carries us, setting the pace.
In the hush of the night, find your seam,
Join in the music of upward dream.

Enchanted Twirl Under the Aurora

Beneath the night's canvas, colors collide,
In a dance of the heavens, where magic resides.
Amidst the cool whispers, the cosmos unfurl,
We twirl in enchantment, a mesmerizing whirl.

With ribbons of light, the sky softly glows,
As laughter of fairies in the stillness flows.
The world is alive, with each twinkling spark,
In this ethereal realm, we leave our mark.

Hand in hand, lost, in the shimmer we sway,
Caught in a trance, as the night turns to day.
In the embrace of the glow, let fears be unfurled,
We weave through the wonders of the enchanted world.

The aurora above, a celestial dance,
In heartbeats and dreams, we find our romance.
Together forever, in this timeless swirl,
We're enchanted to dance under the aurora's pearl.

Celestial Murmurs in the Twilight

As the sun dips low, the stars start to sing,
In the twilight's embrace, the nightbirds take wing.
Soft whispers of cosmos, in breezes they flow,
Brushing past dreams in a gentle tableau.

The horizon blushes, with hues of the night,
In the cradle of dusk, everything feels right.
Each twinkle, a tale, in the silence they weave,
Celestial murmurs that we dare to believe.

Time slows to a hush, in this magical hour,
Where shadows and secrets blend soft as a flower.
With hearts wide open, we listen and vow,
To hold onto glimpses of heaven's own glow.

In the tender embrace of the coming night,
We find in the darkness, an echo of light.
With each star that flickers, in dreams we take flight,
In celestial murmurs, we rise to new heights.

Spiraling Through the Skyscape

On wings of the wind, we gracefully spin,
Where clouds weave their stories, adventure begins.
With laughter of rain, and the sun's tender gaze,
We spiral through layers of sky's soft embrace.

Each turn brings a tale, painted in blue,
In the vastness above, dreams come into view.
The whispers of breezes, the warmth of the day,
Guide us on journeys, where spirits can play.

In the dance of the heavens, we rise and we fall,
Cascading through colors, we feel it all.
A twisting ascent, where freedom awaits,
In spiraling motion, life resonates.

Soaring through passages, both bold and serene,
In the embrace of the air, hear the world's keen.
With eyes open wide, let our souls intertwine,
Spiraling through skyscape, where wonders align.

In the Embrace of Ethereal Light

Underneath the glowing sky,
We dance with shadows, side by side.
Whispers of stars softly sigh,
In their warmth, we confide.

Luminous beams weave through the night,
A tapestry of dreams we weave.
Colors blend, a breathtaking sight,
In this moment, we believe.

Every heartbeat sings a tune,
Carried on the celestial breeze.
Cradled gently by the moon,
As we move with perfect ease.

The universe wraps us tight,
In its arms, forever dear.
Lost within this pure delight,
With each breath, you are near.

Choreography of the Universe

In the vastness, stars align,
A dance of worlds begins to play.
Galaxies swirl, divine design,
In harmony, they always stay.

Planets twirl in perfect grace,
Orbits tracing ancient lines.
Each celestial face a place,
Where time and space intertwines.

Comets glide with fiery trails,
Echoing tales of long-lost nights.
Resounding through the cosmic gales,
The rhythm of celestial flights.

Together they create the tune,
A symphony across the skies.
In the shadows of the moon,
The dance of life forever flies.

Starlit Rhapsodies Above

Whispers travel on the breeze,
Underneath the starlit dome.
In the night, our hearts find ease,
As constellations guide us home.

Each twinkle tells a story, bright,
Of love that spans the void of space.
Weaving dreams in silver light,
In this moment, we embrace.

Nebulae burst in colors bold,
Painting visions on the night.
Secrets in their beauty told,
In their glow, we find delight.

Swaying gently in the dark,
Starlit rhapsodies unfold.
With each note, we leave our mark,
In the cosmos, forever bold.

Poised on the Edge of Infinity

In stillness, we find our place,
On the brink of what could be.
Time expands in endless space,
As we chase eternity.

Glimmers of the future call,
Promises in the silent air.
Together we will risk it all,
For love, a journey we will share.

Eyes reflecting the unknown,
Dreams igniting in the night.
With every breath, the seeds we've sown,
Burst to life in shared delight.

On the edge, we take a chance,
With courage born from deep within.
Together, join the cosmic dance,
Poised on the edge of infinity.

Steps Toward the Infinite Horizon

With every step, the path unfolds,
A whisper of dreams, a tale retold.
Beyond the hills, where sunlight plays,
We chase the dawn of endless days.

Waves of time, in rhythm flow,
Carrying hopes where wild winds blow.
Mountains rise, and valleys sigh,
Beneath the vast, uncharted sky.

Each footprint left, a story spun,
A quest for truth, a race to run.
Through shadows cast by fleeting light,
We wander forth into the night.

As the horizon calls our name,
Embracing all, yet so much the same.
The journey long, the heart feels bold,
In steps toward dreams, our tales unfold.

Enchanted Journeys in Starlit Skies

Under the blanket of midnight hues,
We sail through dreams and morning dews.
Constellations guide our way,
In the hush of night, we gently sway.

Whispers of magic, soft and clear,
In every twinkle, we draw near.
With every wish upon a star,
We soar together, near and far.

The moonlight dances on our skin,
The world asleep, we dive within.
To realms where wonder knows no bounds,
In silence, joy and peace resound.

Through cosmic paths, our spirits play,
In starlit beams, we drift away.
Let time extend and moments freeze,
In enchanted skies, our hearts find ease.

The Cosmic Soiree

Gathered 'round the astral light,
We share our stories of the night.
With laughter bright, our spirits soar,
In the cosmic dance forevermore.

Galaxies twirl, in joyous spin,
While symphonies of stars begin.
Every glance, a secret shared,
In the warmth of love, we are ensnared.

Waltzing through the void, we roam,
In this vast, expanding home.
Echoes of laughter fill the air,
At the table set beneath the flare.

As shadows fade, and dawn peeks in,
We hold our dreams, and let them spin.
In cosmic unity, we sway,
At the soiree where spirits play.

Crescendos of Celestial Laughter

In the halls of stars, we sing aloud,
With voices bold, we draw a crowd.
Each note a spark, each chorus bright,
In the galaxy's embrace, we take flight.

Laughter rings through the space between,
In cosmic rhythms, pure and keen.
From planets close to the distant light,
Our joy resounds through the velvet night.

With every heartbeat, stardust glows,
As together, our melody flows.
In crescendos high, we chase the sound,
In the universe's arms, we are unbound.

As galaxies join in the playful song,
We dance as one, where we belong.
Through laughter's echo, we find our way,
In celestial joy, we choose to stay.

Weightless Whirls on Ethereal Winds

In the gentle breeze we sway,
Floating dreams drift far away.
Whispers of the sky do sing,
Dancing through the air on wing.

Each soft sigh a tale unfolds,
Stories of the days of old.
Carried high, we lose all weight,
In this flight, we celebrate.

Clouds embrace our fleeting flight,
Kissing sun and stars at night.
On this journey, lost in time,
Heart and soul begin to rhyme.

Endless echoes, soft and free,
In the winds, we find our glee.
Weightless, we shall twirl and spin,
In this boundless world, we win.

Tidal Waves of Joy Above the Clouds

Surging waves of laughter rise,
Painting gleams in azure skies.
Hearts unite with joyful sounds,
In this bliss, true love abounds.

Clouds like pillows, soft and white,
Cuddle dreams in morning light.
Float on tides of pure delight,
Heights of joy within our sight.

Each wave crashes with a cheer,
Bringing warmth and drawing near.
An embrace from skies above,
Tidal waves of endless love.

In the rhythm, souls entwined,
All our worries left behind.
Joyful hearts upon the crest,
In this dance, we find our rest.

Spheres of Light in Harmonious Motion

Dancing orbs in radiant glow,
Twirl and spin in endless flow.
Colors blend and intertwine,
In this ballet, worlds align.

Pulse of life in vibrant streams,
Whispers echo our shared dreams.
Each sphere tells a tale untold,
Stories of the brave and bold.

In the dark, they find their way,
Guiding hearts both night and day.
Harmony within the light,
Spheres of hope that banish night.

As they dance, they weave a song,
Every note where we belong.
In this music, joy we find,
Light and love forever bind.

Enlivened by Aurora's Glow

Dawn ignites the sky with fire,
Awakens dreams, ignites desire.
Colors burst in cosmic show,
Hearts are stirred by nature's glow.

Dance of lights upon the night,
Whispers brush with soft delight.
Auroras paint the frozen sky,
In this wonder, spirits fly.

Each shimmer tells a secret tale,
Guiding ships on starlit trail.
Filling eyes with endless grace,
In the glow, we find our place.

Embraced by hues both bright and bold,
Life's sweet stories to unfold.
In this moment, truth we know,
Enlivened by Aurora's glow.

Ballet of the Silver Winds

Whispers dance in twilight's glow,
Gentle breezes start to flow.
Leaves pirouette in whispered glee,
Nature sings a symphony.

Moonlight bathes the earth in grace,
Stars alight in their embrace.
Shadows play on the forest floor,
Echoes of an ancient lore.

Branches sway like waltzing pairs,
Carried high on fragrant airs.
Night unfolds her velvet art,
Each heartbeat, the earth's sweet chart.

In this ballet, all are free,
Lost in dreams of mystery.
Time stands still, a fleeting kiss,
In this dance, a world of bliss.

Floating in Midnight Reverie

Silken waves of night descend,
Stars above like jewels blend.
Drifting on a whisper's sigh,
Where the dreams and shadows lie.

Gentle thoughts in moonlight trace,
Carried forth with tender grace.
In the silence, secrets play,
Softly glowing through ballet.

Time stands still in silver hues,
Wrapped in soft and mystic views.
Floating in this endless sea,
A world spun from reverie.

In a twilight, cool and light,
Hearts ignite in pure delight.
Each moment, a cherished thread,
In this dance where spirits tread.

Steps Between the Stars

Underneath the cosmic arch,
Footsteps trace a silent march.
In this vast and endless space,
Dreamers find their sacred place.

With each step, the stardust glows,
Mapping out where magic flows.
Constellations guide the way,
In the light of night and day.

Floating soft on lunar beams,
Wandering through time and dreams.
Here in light, our spirits soar,
Endless paths forevermore.

Galaxies in colors swirl,
In this dance, we spin and twirl.
Steps we take in twilight's arms,
Wrapped in night's celestial charms.

Cloudborne Dreams Unfurled

High above in skies so bright,
Clouds weave stories in the light.
Whispers drift on airy wings,
Unseen magic life brings.

Each puff paints a tale anew,
Softly kissed by morning dew.
In this realm where visions shine,
Dreams take flight on threads divine.

Floating high on breezes sweet,
Every heart finds its own beat.
Time is lost in gentle flow,
Where the wildest dreams can grow.

Cloudborne fantasies arise,
In the sun's embracing skies.
From the heights, our thoughts set free,
In this dance, eternity.

Ethereal Euphoria in the Abyss

In shadows deep, where silence reigns,
A glimmer shines, in subtle chains.
Soft whispers call from realms unseen,
Euphoria born in twilight's sheen.

Beneath the waves of darkened night,
Hope flickers faint, yet holds so bright.
A dance of stars in endless sky,
In hidden depths, our spirits fly.

From depths of sorrow, joy will bloom,
In tranquil peace, we find our room.
Lost in the void, yet never alone,
In abyss's heart, we make our home.

With every breath, the cosmos sings,
Ethereal dreams on angel's wings.
A melody sways, transcending time,
In the abyss, love's pulse sublime.

Cosmic Steps of Infinite Wonder

Footprints traced on starlit floors,
Beyond the realms, where silence soars.
Galaxies swirl in timeless grace,
Each step reveals a sacred place.

Wonders vast, like oceans spread,
In cosmic dance, our hearts are led.
The pulse of life, from stardust spun,
In every heartbeat, we are one.

Through nebulae, our spirits glide,
On waves of light, we gently ride.
Infinite paths, like whispers flow,
Into the dark, our dreams shall glow.

In this ballet of space and time,
The universe sings in perfect rhyme.
With every step, a spark ignites,
The wonder ceaseless, in endless nights.

Veils of Laughter in the Atmosphere

Laughter floats through misty air,
A melody light, for hearts to share.
With every giggle, worries cease,
In joyous notes, we find our peace.

Veils of joy, like petals fall,
Whispering secrets that call us all.
In playful breezes, spirits soar,
Together we laugh, forevermore.

Beneath the sky, so vast and blue,
The world a stage, for me and you.
In joyful moments, life feels right,
We dance through days, wrapped in sheer light.

The echoes linger, soft and sweet,
As laughter weaves a bond complete.
In every heartbeat, love takes flight,
Veils of laughter glow through the night.

The Elysian Dance of Mavericks

In fields of dreams, the mavericks roam,
With courage fierce, they carve their home.
Every step, a rhythm bold,
In Elysian realms, their truths unfold.

Stars align in vibrant hues,
As daring hearts break classic views.
They twirl and leap, defy the norm,
In joyous chaos, new worlds form.

Through trials faced, their spirits rise,
With laughter rich, they touch the skies.
Each twirl a tale, each leap a song,
In dance of life, where all belong.

Together they move, in perfect grace,
The Mavericks shine in this sacred space.
With every heartbeat, they redefine,
The essence of life, in love entwined.

Lullabies of the Ether

In whispers soft, the stars do sing,
A melody of peace they bring.
Where shadows dance in silver light,
Lullabies weave through the night.

The gentle breeze through leaves does flow,
Carrying dreams on wings of glow.
Every sigh and every sigh,
Sings a tune to the night sky.

Here, in stillness, we softly drift,
Held in the arms of cosmic gift.
Among the echoes, hearts align,
Floating in love, so divine.

So lay your head and close your eyes,
Hear the songs of starlit skies.
In this space, where dreams take flight,
Lullabies cradle us tonight.

Twirling in the Moonbeam's Embrace

Underneath the silver glow,
We twirl where softer breezes blow.
Moonbeams wrap us, warm and bright,
Guiding us through the velvet night.

In this dance, the world feels small,
With whispers sweet, we hear the call.
Stars twinkle to our gentle sway,
Carrying our hearts away.

Embracing shadows, we find our way,
Lost in the music, night turns to day.
Each spin a promise, each step a dream,
Together we flow with the moon's soft beam.

Time stands still in this sacred place,
Here we find our endless grace.
With every laugh, we claim our space,
Twirling in the moonbeam's embrace.

Swaying Among the Nebulas

In the depths of night's embrace,
We sway in a cosmic grace.
Nebulas swirl in colors bright,
A tapestry woven with starlight.

Floating gently, we lose the ground,
In this harmony, love is found.
Every hue tells a story new,
Guided by the dreams we pursue.

With open hearts, we drift along,
Carried by the universe's song.
In the silence, our spirits sing,
Swaying as one on celestial wing.

Let the galaxies spin and twine,
In this dance, your heart is mine.
Among the stars, we find our place,
Swaying among the nebulas with grace.

Rhythms of the Celestial Sphere

In the vast expanse where stars collide,
A rhythm beats with every tide.
Planets turn in a cosmic dance,
Drawing us into a timeless trance.

Whispers of galaxies fill the air,
Echoes of love dance everywhere.
With every pulse, the universe grows,
In the heart of night, our spirit glows.

We find our harmony, lost in the rhyme,
Every moment a gift, a pause in time.
Resonate with the cosmos in view,
Rhythms of the heart, pure and true.

So let's twine our souls, forever bound,
To the rhythm of life, a sacred sound.
Together we'll move, forever near,
In the rhythms of the celestial sphere.

Lightning Bug Lullabies

In the quiet of night, they glow,
Tiny lanterns with a soft show.
Whispers of magic dance in air,
Bringing peace, without a care.

They flicker bright, like stars in flight,
Underneath the crescent light.
Nature's whispers, soft and sweet,
Carry dreams on gentle beat.

Children listen, eyes all aglow,
As the fireflies put on their show.
Swaying softly to night's embrace,
Finding warmth in this sacred space.

With each blink, a soft lullaby,
Telling secrets to the sky.
In their glow, we find our rest,
Wrapped in dreams, we feel so blessed.

Celestial Shimmers in Spirals

Stars spiral high in cosmic dance,
Twinkling bright, they captivate a glance.
Galaxies swirl in colors bold,
Ancient stories of beauty told.

Nebulae paint the heavens bright,
With whispers of creation's light.
Each shimmer tells a tale untold,
In the canvas of the night so cold.

Planets waltz in silent grace,
In the vastness, we find our place.
A shimmer here, a spiral yonder,
Wondering how we came to ponder.

In this realm, all dreams take flight,
Beneath the moon, we feel so right.
Celestial wonders, oh so near,
In spirals, we shed each fear.

Fantasia Under the Cosmic Canopy

Underneath the stars so bright,
We weave dreams of pure delight.
The cosmic quilt wraps us tight,
In a symphony of night.

Galactic whispers fill the air,
Filling hearts with tender care.
Dancing shadows, soft and free,
In this enchanted tapestry.

Shooting stars ignite the sky,
Painting wishes as they fly.
A canvas rich, a vibrant hue,
In this realm where dreams come true.

Fantasia sings a lullaby,
Underneath the endless sky.
With every beat, our spirits soar,
In this magic, we explore.

Clouds Embracing Starlight

Softly drifting, clouds in flight,
Caressing whispers of starlight.
Together they dance, a gentle sweep,
Where the night unfolds its secret keep.

Silver threads of twilight glow,
Nestled in the night's soft flow.
Stars peek through, a playful game,
In this dreamscape, nothing's the same.

Clouds embrace the starlit beams,
Cradling the world in silver dreams.
A tender hug from skies above,
Filling hearts with gentle love.

As night stretches, we find our peace,
Beneath the clouds, our worries cease.
Together, they weave a soft embrace,
In a cosmic ballet, we find our place.

Swaying with the Auroral Breeze

Dancing lights paint the night sky,
Whispers of colors, soft and spry.
The world is still, yet alive,
As shadows and glows sweetly dive.

Gentle winds weave through the trees,
Carrying secrets, like a tease.
Nature's hymn calls out to me,
In the night's embrace, I feel free.

Stars twinkle like distant dreams,
Flowing through time, or so it seems.
Each breeze a brush, each spark a sigh,
In this moment, I learn to fly.

Together we sway, hand in hand,
Lost in the rhythm, understand.
With the auroral dance tonight,
Our spirits soar, hearts full of light.

When Dreams Unfurl Their Wings

In the silence of the night,
Whispers urge us to take flight.
VEils of stardust greet our eyes,
As we ascend beyond the skies.

Ideas bloom like flowers bright,
Filling our hearts with sheer delight.
Imaginations rise and fall,
As dreams unfurl, we hear the call.

Guided by the moon's soft glow,
Through the stardust, we will go.
Every hope ignites a spark,
Leading us through the endless dark.

Together we chase these visions bold,
A tapestry of stories told.
When dreams take flight on gossamer wings,
We dance in the light of what tomorrow brings.

Lifting Spirits on Silken Currents

Gentle waves caress the shore,
Each ripple calls for something more.
Carried high on liquid dreams,
Life flows sweet, or so it seems.

Tides of change pull hearts along,
In the surge, we find our song.
In drops of joy, let laughter sing,
As we embrace the love they bring.

Floating softly on the air,
Chasing moments, light as a prayer.
Every whisper, every gleam,
Guides us towards our shared dream.

On currents fine, our spirits soar,
Finding wings, we long for more.
Together in this dance of fate,
We lift our dreams, it's never too late.

In the Presence of Celestial Grace

Beneath the vast and starry dome,
A world awakens, far from home.
With every twinkle, every spark,
A tapestry woven deep in the dark.

Time unfolds in silent hues,
We're cradled in the night's soft muse.
In presence sweet, we find our place,
Bathed in the glow of celestial grace.

Hearts entwined beneath the sky,
A bond unbroken, we learn to fly.
Guided by light—the way is clear,
Each moment we share, we hold dear.

As galaxies dance, we too sway,
Together we dream, come what may.
In the night's stillness, we embrace,
All that we hold in this sacred space.

Echoes of Liquid Light

Whispers of dawn in liquid gold,
Shimmering waves in stories untold.
Reflecting dreams on the surface bright,
Dancing softly, they weave through the night.

Ripples of time in the silence flow,
Carving paths where the wildflowers grow.
Each drop a memory, a moment's glance,
Inviting the heart to join in the dance.

Colors of twilight spread wide and far,
Beneath the glow of the evening star.
Echoes linger where shadows reside,
Carried away on the ebb of the tide.

Lost in the movement, a soothing embrace,
Nature's canvas, a tranquil space.
In every shimmer, a story untold,
Awakening dreams that brightly unfold.

Tracing the Edges of Infinity

In the silence where shadows appear,
Time bends softly, and whispers draw near.
A dance of the cosmos, vast and profound,
Seeking the borders where dreams can be found.

Stars scattered like seeds in the night,
Painting the heavens with shimmering light.
Each point a promise, a path to explore,
Unlocking the mysteries forevermore.

The universe hums in a cosmic tune,
Beneath the gaze of the watchful moon.
In the spiral of galaxies, we find our way,
Tracing the edges where shadows play.

Journeying onward, through space and through time,
We dance in the echoes, both rhythm and rhyme.
A quest for the infinite, boundless and free,
Where all that we are is just meant to be.

Leap Into the Celestial Ballet

In the velvet sky, the stars take flight,
A ballet of worlds, a dazzling sight.
Twinkling dancers in patterns divine,
Each leap a whisper of the cosmic design.

Galaxies swirling in unison's grace,
Embracing the heavens in timeless space.
With every excursion through the vast night,
We lose ourselves in the brilliance of light.

Planets pirouette on orbits so grand,
Moving in harmony, hand in hand.
As comets streak past like fleeting dreams,
The universe pulses with radiant beams.

Together we leap, in celestial flow,
In awe of the wonders the cosmos bestow.
The choreographed dance, a sight to behold,
Takes us beyond to the stories retold.

A Choreography of Starlight

Dancing on whispers of fate and design,
Stars weave their stories in patterns divine.
Each twinkle a promise, each glow a refrain,
In the great cosmic dance, we lose all disdain.

Moonlight pirouettes on the waters below,
Casting reflections where dreams freely flow.
With each gentle step, we join in the sway,
In the arms of the night, we find our way.

Nebulae cradle the secrets of time,
In colors so vibrant, they shimmer and shine.
A choreography written in light's gentle hand,
Guiding our spirits through celestial strands.

In the tapestry woven by luminous threads,
We move with the echoes, where starlight spreads.
Lost in the music of the galaxies' play,
Together we dance till the break of the day.

Reveries of the Misty Heights

In the morning glow, dreams entwined,
Whispers of clouds, sweet secrets I find.
Mountains stand tall, with heads in the skies,
Echoes of silence, where the heart lies.

Soft shadows dance, with a delicate grace,
Misty veils wrap, every familiar place.
Footsteps untraced, on the dew-kissed ground,
In the realm of dreams, I am forever bound.

Glimmers of hope, in the soft light appear,
Every breath taken, drawing you near.
Time slips away, like sand through my hands,
In these reveries, a love that expands.

As night descends, stars twinkle above,
Cradled in stillness, my heart is in love.
With the mist, I wander, forever entwined,
In these heights of wonder, peace I find.

Waltz of Glittering Horizons

The sun takes its bow, in a golden embrace,
Waves in rhythm, a celestial grace.
Colors ignite, like a dancer's flair,
On the horizon, dreams heed the air.

Each twinkle a promise, a tale to unfold,
With echoes of laughter, and stories retold.
The night calls to life, with its silvery hue,
In the waltz of the stars, I find you anew.

Time swirls like a breeze, dancing through space,
In the arms of the twilight, we find our place.
Every moment a treasure, each heartbeat a song,
In this glittering waltz, we both belong.

As the moon takes its throne, casting dreams wide,
Through the shadows we glide, side by side.
The night is our canvas, painted with light,
In this dance of horizons, everything feels right.

Movements Above the Horizon

Clouds drift softly, painting skies anew,
A canvas of dreams, in every shade and hue.
Whispers of winds carry tales from afar,
In movements of grace, like a guiding star.

With each passing moment, the world comes alive,
Nature's orchestra plays, in harmony we thrive.
Birds take to flight, in a choreographed dance,
Above the horizon, we seize every chance.

The sunset ignites, in a fiery embrace,
Filling the horizon with a warm, tender grace.
Each shadow that lengthens tells stories untold,
In movements above, watch the wonders unfold.

As the dusk settles in, and darkness begins,
A new rhythm emerges, a symphony spins.
In the stillness of night, dreams take their flight,
These movements above, lead us into the light.

Kites of Fantasia in the Breeze

Kites soar high, in a laughter-filled sky,
Colors unfurl, as the breezes fly by.
With each gust of wind, tales take to flight,
In this realm of wonder, hearts feel so light.

Strings intertwined, like destinies spun,
In the game of the winds, we become one.
Chasing the clouds, in a joyful embrace,
Every twist and turn, a beautiful chase.

The sun kisses fabric, igniting the bright,
As dreams in the air turn day into night.
Whispers of freedom ride high on the breeze,
In this dance of kites, we find sweet ease.

With laughter and joy, we float and we dare,
Creating our worlds, drifting without care.
In this fantasia, our spirits are free,
Kites in the breeze, it's just you and me.

Milton Keynes UK
Ingram Content Group UK Ltd.
UKHW021628011224
451755UK00010B/515